Take Care of Yourself

Staying Safe with
Technology

by Ashley Richardson

PEBBLE
a capstone imprint

Published by Pebble, an imprint of Capstone.
1710 Roe Crest Drive, North Mankato, Minnesota 56003
capstonepub.com

Library of Congress Cataloging-in-Publication Data is available on the Library of Congress website.
ISBN 9781663976789 (hardcover)
ISBN 9781666326994 (paperback)
ISBN 9781666327007 (ebook pdf)

Summary: Readers will learn ways to stay safe while using technology and important steps to take if they run into problems. Includes a hands-on activity.

Image Credits
Capstone Studio: Karon Dubke, 7, 8, 13; Getty Images: FatCamera, 6, FilippoBacci, 14, monkeybusinessimages, 15, Shelyna Long, 16; Shutterstock: Anna Golant (design element) throughout, Annashou, 20 (left), fizkes, 5, GaudiLab, 9, JuliyaShangarey, 17, LightField Studios, 19, Monkey Business Images, 18, myboys.me, Cover, Parinya Maneenate, 11, ravl, 20 (right)

Editorial Credits
Editor: Erika L. Shores; Designer: Heidi Thompson; Media Researcher: Jo Miller; Production Specialist: Tori Abraham

All internet sites appearing in back matter were available and accurate when this book was sent to press.

Printed and bound in the USA. PO4608

Table of Contents

Words in **bold** are in the glossary.

Technology and You

Did you read a book on a tablet today? Maybe you video chatted with a friend. If so, you used technology.

Technology lets you **interact** with the world. You can go **online** to connect with family and friends. Online games and videos are fun to play and watch. You use the internet to find answers to questions. You likely use technology every day.

Staying Safe Online

The internet is full of **information**. Websites and games help you learn. You can find funny pictures or cool videos. But sometimes what you find online can be unsafe or untrue.

Online videos or pictures can be scary.

You might read mean comments on a **post**.

What should you do? Trust your feelings.

Talk to a trusted grown-up to help decide

if what you saw was even real or true.

Follow the Rules

Rules about using technology help keep you safe. Teachers and parents may tell you to only visit certain websites. Maybe you're only allowed to chat online with kids from your school.

You want to play a new game online. You want to share a photo. An **app** is asking you to buy something. Stop! Ask a trusted adult first. Never share or buy anything online without asking.

Avoid Strangers

People you don't know may try to talk to you online. They might ask your name and where you live. They might want to know your age and school. You would never get in a car with a stranger. So, you should never talk to one online.

Sometimes websites or apps will ask for personal information. Never share your name, age, or address without asking a trusted adult first.

Remember to always trust your feelings. Did someone send you a message that makes you feel bad? Did someone ask you a personal question in a chat? Do you feel unsure if someone is who they say they are online? Trust your gut. Only use technology to talk to people you know in real life.

Be Kind Online

Sometimes technology can be used to say or do mean things. Did someone write something mean during an online game? Or send a hurtful message? Trying to hurt someone's feelings online is called **cyberbullying**. This behavior is never OK.

Talk to people online the way you would in real life. Be kind. Remember someone is on the other side of the screen. Someone just like you!

15

What do you do if someone online is mean to you? Take a deep breath. Don't **respond** right away. Tell someone you trust. This person can help you find a solution.

Think about cyberbullying in the same way as bullying at school. Be brave. Speak out! And ask for help from a grown-up.

Staying Balanced

Technology helps us learn and have fun. But we can spend too much time online. Do different things during your day. Read. Paint. Run.

Spending too much time online can hurt **relationships**. You may have less time for fun with friends and family. Keep relationships strong by spending time together.

Make Your Own Game

Board games are a fun way to spend time with family and friends. You can create your own!

What You Need:

- sturdy paper, such as poster board or cardboard
- drawing supplies, such as markers or colored pencils
- small objects to use as game pieces, such as buttons, Lego bricks, or small rocks
- dice

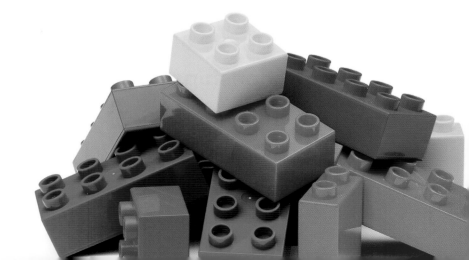

What You Do:

1. Pick a theme for your game. Will your board game be an underwater adventure? Will it be based on your favorite movie?
2. Make the board. Draw a winding path for the pieces to move around. Where does the game start? Where does it end?
3. Make the rules. Will your game have cards with challenges and rewards? For example, one card might say, *Go back five spaces.*
4. Roll the dice to move the game pieces.
5. Ask neighbors, friends, or family members to play your game!

Glossary

app (AP)—a useful program that is downloaded to computers and mobile devices; app is short for application

cyberbullying (SY-buhr-bul-ee-ing)—the act of bullying someone by posting mean or threatening messages about the person online

information (in-fur-MAY-shuhn)—knowledge that you get about someone or something; facts or details about a subject

interact (in-tur-AKT)—to have action between people, groups, or things

online (ON-LAYN)—connected to the internet

post (POHST)—something put online meant for other people to see or read

relationship (re-LAY-shun-ship)—the way two or more people or things are connected

respond (re-SPAHND)—to say something in return

Read More

Matteson, Adrienne. *Staying Safe Online*. Ann Arbor, MI: Cherry Lake Publishing, 2020.

Shofner, Melissa Raé. *Protecting Personal Information.* New York: PowerKids Press, 2019.

Internet Sites

Kids' Rules for Online Safety
safekids.com/kids-rules-for-online-safety

Ruff Ruffman: Privacy and You!
pbslearningmedia.org/resource/ruff16-pd-privacy/
wgbh-ruff-ruffman-privacy-and-you

Index

About the Author

Ashley Richardson writes fiction, poetry, and creative nonfiction. She enjoys reading all kinds of books and lives in the Midwest with a houseful of plants. For fun, Ashley loves to inline skate in the park.